MENTES
LIBRES

ELIMINATES ANXIETY AND PANIC ATTACKS

INDEX

Chapter 1: Anxiety - What is it?

Your heart is pounding and you feel dizzy. It feels like you have to sit down so you don't fall. You have trouble catching your breath. You are experiencing a numbing sensation in your hands and feet.

There's a pressure in the chest area. You think you may be on the verge of a heart attack. You think something is really wrong with you; however, you are far from dead.

Anxiety is a mental disorder in which a person fears almost anything and thinks all the results will be worse. This fear is frightening because it is so intense and they are always afraid that someone will come after them.

If you have some kind of disorder associated with anxiety, then your mind will always be focused on being scared for no reason. You will always feel that there is no solution to your unfounded fear and that there is no way out.

You feel paralyzed as if there is nothing you can do. Basically, you are frozen in fear. This disorder can strike at any time.

Anxiety disorder is more than an action. Anxiety disorder has different subtleties that can fit into this. For example, there are panic attacks, obsessive-compulsive disorder, and others that are related to the anxiety disorder family.

There are many people everywhere who suffer from anxiety attacks. If you're not affected by them, you may know someone who is. If it's you, you need to know how to help yourself. If it's someone else, you need to know how to help them. You'll need to be supportive and help them get the treatment and support they need to fight this condition.

Chapter 2: Causes of Anxiety

There is not one single thing that causes this disorder and those related to it. You may think there are certain things that trigger it. Well, there could be, and again, it could be something that just happens. It all depends on how it's perceived.

Those who have anxiety attacks or related disorders may have an attack. Then they may return to the scene where the initial one took place and have another one. They are reminded of what happened before. They will feel bad and end up having another one without thinking about it. It seems like a constant cycle of intense fear. Then they feel like they will have more attacks.

Believe it or not, it's all in the mind. If they constantly fear and expect to have an anxiety attack or something related to it, then it will happen. What happens is that people who experience these attacks resent hearing that everything is in the mind. They feel that people forget this as something that can be overcome.

The feeling of anxiety comes from your brain. According to studies that deal with this, there are at least two areas of the brain that help trigger the feeling of fear and anxiety in the mind. This gives your brain a defense mechanism and then you react.

However, there may be situations that you may think cause anxiety and related attacks. Some people have a lot of stress these days. It can come from office politics, overwhelming debt, family problems, and other events that can cause this.

There are also some medications that can trigger an anxiety attack because of side effects or withdrawal. These include alcohol, caffeine, cold medicines, decongestants, nicotine, diet pills, and many other medicines that people take for various illnesses and diseases.

Not eating well can also contribute to anxiety. There are some situations where you may have to take a test or deal with a lot of people. If you're not prepared, you may become nervous or shaky.

Chapter 3: Who suffers from anxiety?

There is no particular group on this earth that is a target of anxiety and related attacks or disorders. So, that said, who do you think suffers from this? Well, it could be anyone. It could be in your family, your friends, co-workers, or anyone you know.

Many times, it could be those you know and never would have thought in a million years that they would suffer from something like this.

Unfortunately, these attacks are often kept

secret and not disclosed. This is one of those embarrassing "sweeping under the rug" moments. It's not something you talk about openly. Some people will recognize that they are dealing with this when they are caught in the act and cannot fake it.

Believe it or not, there are people like politicians and even Hollywood celebrities who suffer from anxiety attacks and related conditions. However, they pay their advertisers and others not to see it.

They don't want to be in the spotlight because they have to work to maintain their image. What they don't realize, however, is that someone may benefit from their exposure.

Unfortunately, for people who have to deal with this, anxiety attacks affect and tend to interfere with those who are trying to live a normal life. If you are having excessive anxiety attacks, it may be related to a psychiatric condition. When these attacks become severe and last a long time, they are considered out of the norm.

With the symptoms of an anxiety attack, the brain transmits messages to other parts of the person's body. Certain parts of the body, such as the lungs and heart, work overtime while an anxiety attack occurs. The brain ends up releasing a lot of adrenaline.

Chapter 4: Other Forms of Anxiety Attacks/Disorders

Generalized Anxiety Disorder (GAD)

Generalized anxiety disorder, or GAD, deals with people who are constantly worried and always tense. The point is that there really isn't a cause for this, nor is anyone or anything to blame for causing it. They look for the worst and are always extremely worried about work, family health, and money. They even feel anxiety in the course of their normal day.

If this pattern is consistent for at least six

months, a person can be considered to have GAD. They feel that they can't stop worrying even if the worry isn't as great as they seem.

It is difficult for them to relax, they are easily startled by people or noises, and they have difficulty concentrating.   Sometimes they can't sleep at night or wake up in the morning by themselves.   These are some other symptoms that contribute to GAD:

- Feeling tired
- Pain in the muscles
- Irritable
- Nausea
- Sweaty
- Shortness of breath
- Frequent trips to the bathroom
- Tremor, palpitation

- The hot flashes

If they do not have a high level of anxiety and continue to suffer from GAD, they may continue to work and be able to interact socially with others. However, if they have GAD on a higher scale, they may have trouble doing and completing simple tasks that others would take for granted.

About seven million American adults have GAD. More women (about twice as many) are dealing with it than men. Still, the risk peaks from childhood to the middle years. Studies have shown that there are some genes that contribute to people getting GAD.

There are other anxiety disorders that occur along with GAD, such as substance abuse and depression. If treated properly, a person can overcome his or her concerns with any problems he or she has.

Social Anxiety Disorder

Social anxiety disorder, also known as social phobia, occurs when a person is extremely self-conscious and anxious. It occurs every day in different social situations. They are very afraid of being watched.

They are also afraid of being judged by others. They try to be extremely careful and try hard not to do things that might cause them embarrassment.

For a while, they are extremely fearful before

a situation they feel may turn into a disaster. It can become so bad that they lose concentration and cannot think clearly. With social anxiety disorder, they may let this fear cause them to lose their concentration.

It doesn't matter if it happens at school, work, or home. Having a social anxiety disorder can make it hard for a person to cultivate relationships with others.

With social anxiety disorder, it can be hard for people to overcome their excessive fears and worries. This is true even if they know that what they're feeling isn't realistic. Some will try to make amends.

Even then, there's a sense of anxiety, and they don't feel comfortable being around other people. Then they worry too much about how others thought of them after the encounter.

A person may be in a social setting (for example, at dinner with someone or with more than one person) and will experience anxiety because they are afraid. They will sweat a lot, blush, shake, or have difficulty having a conversation with other people at the table. They always seem to feel that other people are watching them.

Millions of adults have social anxiety disorder, or social phobia. For the most part, this condition begins in childhood and may continue into adolescence.

There are some studies that say genetics play

a role in this. This condition is often accompanied by depression or other anxiety disorders or attacks. It is not a good idea for those affected to treat themselves with medication. It could make the situation worse. This is best treated by professionals who have experience in this field.

Obsessive Compulsive Disorder

People dealing with obsessive-compulsive disorder, or OCD, constantly have thoughts that can make them angry. To control their anxiety, they use compulsions (rituals). However, the tables end up turning on them because the rituals take over their minds.

For example, there are some people who are obsessed with cleanliness. They are known as "cleanliness phenomena. Of course, it's good practice to want everything to be kept clean, but they can get too close to controlling germs or dirty surfaces.

They have a compulsion to wash their hands continuously. They don't want any germs or dirt to touch their hands. When they go to the bathroom, they take a paper towel to open and close the door, just to keep germs from getting on their hands.

If people with OCD don't feel like they look good, they'll look in the mirror several times until they feel presentable. They don't want to feel as if they look out of place among others.

These actions provide a temporary release

from the anxiety they have been feeling. People with this disorder are always forced to check things over and over again, or to make sure things are in the same place repeatedly.

Sometimes, they are obsessed with ideas of violence or harm to others. They also have thoughts of crazy things that people wouldn't normally think about. There are times when they feel they have to hoard and store things they don't need.

There are some who have rituals in their home. One of the most common is to check the stove several times before you go out to make sure it is turned off. Having an obsessive-compulsive disorder can become chaotic and an unwanted interruption when it happens every day.

When a person has OCD, he or she knows that what he or she is doing doesn't make much sense, but doesn't see his or her behavior as abnormal.

There are more than two million adults in the United States who have obsessive-compulsive disorder. This condition doesn't stand out by itself. It can be combined with things like anxiety disorders or attacks, depression, or eating disorders.

This disorder affects women and men almost equally. It usually begins in childhood or may begin in adolescence or even adulthood. Research suggests that OCD may be caused by genetics. At least one-third of all adults in the United States start OCD in childhood.

The symptoms of OCD can come and go at any time. If it really gets worse, it can seriously affect a person by acting in a normal capacity and performing certain tasks. It is a good idea for those dealing with it not to use alcohol or drugs to calm them down. It only makes the situation worse for them.

There are certain treatments and medications that can be used to prevent obsessive-compulsive disorder. They can help people who are afraid or anxious to become desensitized to what is going on around them.

Post-Traumatic Stress Disorder

Post-Traumatic Stress Disorder or PTSD occurs when someone has suffered something that involves damage to the body or involves the threat of damage. The person suffering from PTSD may have been harmed, or it may have been someone close to them.

PTSD is commonly known in relation to veterans who served in a war. However, there are other things, such as rape, kidnapping, abuse, car accidents, plane crashes, or natural disasters like hurricanes or floods.

Those who suffer from PTSD can easily become frightened. They also feel nothing for those they used to have a close relationship with. They begin to have less interest in the things they used to do. They show less affection, are increasingly aggressive and show more of an irritable side.

They try to block out the things that remind them of that traumatic event instead of working on it. If the event was something someone else deliberately acted out against them, then PTSD will affect them greatly.

Nightmares can haunt them and they begin to see flashbacks such as sounds, feelings, and images of what happened. There are sounds that can remind them of that event. For example, if a door slams shut, that can mean someone has you trapped in a room and ready to pounce on you with their abuse.

It could be by physical or verbal means. Some people don't realize that verbal abuse is as bad, if not worse, than physical abuse.

Keep in mind that all people who have been traumatized will not experience PTSD. Some people are able to cope with what happened and move on. Others need therapy and medication to deal with their problems.

PTSD can start a few months after the event or incident. It may last a few more months, or continue through the years. To be officially classified as PTSD, symptoms must continue for at least one month. There are some who end up having PTSD as a chronic condition.

There are over millions of adults who are dealing with Post-Traumatic Stress Disorder. It can begin in childhood and continue into adulthood. More women suffer from it than men. PTSD is also combined with substance abuse, depression or other disorders or anxiety attacks.

Chapter 5: Panic Disorder and Panic Attacks

Panic disorder is considered a disease. Symptoms include the feeling of sudden terror, the sensation of fainting, chest pain, or the feeling of suffocation. Panic attacks fall under the condition of panic disorder and are prone to some of these same symptoms, in addition to others. When someone has a panic attack, there are thoughts that are unrealistic or fearful that they are no longer under control or a situation.

With panic disorder, a person may also experience depression or substance abuse. If these conditions are linked to your panic disorder, they should not be treated together. Sometimes they will feel sad or not want to eat. They may not be able to sleep or may only sleep a few hours. They don't have much energy to do anything and can't keep their concentration.

Panic Attack

A panic attack is when a person has a fear or apprehension that is sudden or intense. Usually there is nothing wrong and no one is in danger. Panic attacks can occur suddenly, last a few minutes, and then stop. There are others that last longer than a few minutes or there may be more than one and they follow one another.

There are three types of panic attacks:

- Spontaneous: These panic attacks occur without warning. There is nothing that can provoke them. Even if a person is sleeping, they may experience a panic attack.

- Situational: These panic attacks occur when there is a situation to which a person has been or will be exposed. They are considered to trigger or provoke the panic attack. For example, if a person hears a car backfiring, it might remind them of when they were in the military and fighting a war with ammunition.

- Predisposed to the situation: These panic attacks can occur when there is a delayed reaction. The attack does not always occur immediately. There are some cases where people may have an attack immediately, and other cases where it is delayed or may not occur at all.

Panic attacks are defined as having at least four or more symptoms:

- A choking feeling
- Dizzy or upset
- Shaken
- Tremors
- Shortness of breath
- The acceleration of the heartbeat
- Chest pain
- Numbness

- Chills
- Feeling of going crazy
- Nausea
- Sweating
- Feelings of detachment

If a person experiences fewer than four symptoms, it can still be classified as having a panic attack, but it would be called a "limited-symptom" panic attack. A person can have a panic attack at any time. It can even occur when they are sleeping. It has affected millions of adults.

However, more women are experiencing panic attacks. In fact, women experience panic attacks twice as often as men. Panic attacks can begin in late adolescence or early adulthood.

Some people have frequent panic attacks and are left almost helpless. There are some places they will have to stay away from because it can trigger another attack.

Or a person may not be able to participate in some activities, such as shopping and related outings. Most of the time, they are confined to the place where they live and will not go out unless someone else is with them.

This condition is called agoraphobia, which is when a person is afraid of open spaces or being alone. If they seek help in time for this, progressive treatment can be successful.

It is a very treatable anxiety disorder and will

respond to most medications or therapies provided. Medication and/or therapy can help the affected person alter his or her thinking to get rid of the fear and anxiety.

If you have frequent panic attacks, you may have a panic disorder. Panic attacks become a panic disorder when the condition becomes chronic. Your life can be in serious danger, along with other people's lives.

Chapter 6: Getting Help

If you think you may be experiencing symptoms of an anxiety disorder, a seizure or a related condition, please consult your doctor. He or she will be able to advise you if your symptoms match the clinical diagnosis of any of these mental health conditions.

If so, you should consult with a professional who specializes in mental health conditions. These professionals are trained in therapies that deal with various patterns of behavior and will suggest medications if warranted.

Find one that you are comfortable talking to about your condition. You don't want to be intimidated by their presence. You want to be relaxed and able to discuss what's going on with you. Your mental health professional will work with you to come up with a plan to help you get through your struggles with these types of disorders and attacks.

If you are prescribed medication, you should take it as directed and not stop unless your doctor tells you to. You and your mental health professional or doctor should discuss how the medication will work. If you have side effects, please discuss them as soon as possible. They may have altered your dosage.

As for the cost of medication and treatment, most insurance plans will cover it. However, do not assume this and check with your insurance company first. If you don't have insurance, check with your local or national government agency to seek mental health care at one of their facilities.

Government agencies usually stick to a sliding scale, depending on how much you can afford. Or if you have public assistance, it can help pay for these services.

Chapter 7: Medication and Treatment

For the most part, medications are used for anxiety attacks, disorders, and related conditions. Options may depend on the condition and what the person wants. A doctor should perform a complete evaluation to determine if you are actually suffering from one of these mental health conditions.

If so, he or she should also establish what type of disorder he or she is treating. If there is a combination of things, they should also be identified so that the doctor knows how to treat it.

If you've already been treated for an existing or past anxiety disorder, your doctor should know about it. He or she also needs to know if the medication has been given and the dose.

Or if they have received other treatment, that should be disclosed as well. If there were any side effects, that should be included, along with any therapy that was provided and whether it was beneficial to them.

There are some people who feel that the treatment they received did not work for them. Sometimes, they may not have had enough time for the process to change or it may not have been done correctly. Some people may have to go through different medications or treatments to find what works for them.

Medication is not the ultimate cure for anxiety disorders, seizures, and related conditions. However, medication can control these conditions while the person is receiving therapy. Medication can only be used if a doctor prescribes it.

They are usually prescribed by psychiatrists who offer work therapy with colleagues who provide some of the same services. Most medications used for anxiety disorders are

- Antidepressants
- Anti-anxiety drugs
- Beta-blockers

Using any of these medications can help a person lead a normal life.

Antidepressants

Originally, antidepressants were used for the treatment of depression. However, they also work for those who suffer from anxiety disorders. They work to change brain chemistry. Once the initial dose is taken, it takes at least 4-6 weeks before symptoms disappear. The medication must be taken as directed for this to work.

SSRIs - Selective Serotonin Reuptake Inhibitors: These antidepressants work to change the level of communication in brain cells. Some of the most common are Prozac, Zoloft, and Lexapro.

They are used to treat any panic disorder that is mixed with social phobia, depression, or obsessive-compulsive disorder. Because they are newer, they don't have as many side effects. However, those who use them may experience nervousness or nausea in the early stages of use. This is only temporary.

Tricyclics: These antidepressants are older than the SSRIs and are used for anxiety disorders other than OCD. They are given in low doses and gradually increased.

Side effects include dizziness, dry mouth, drowsiness, and weight gain. This can be eliminated by adjusting the dose or using another medication from the same type of antidepressant. Tofranil is used for GAD and panic disorder; anafranil is used for OCD.

MAOI-Monoamine Oxidase Inhibitors: These are the oldest antidepressants that can be used for these conditions. It is mostly used for anxiety disorders, seizures, and related conditions.

Some of the most common are Nardil, Marplan, and Parnate. When taking MAOIs, there are certain foods and drinks to stay away from. These include cheese and red wine.

Besides that, you can't take Advil, Motrin, Tylenol, or any other pain, cold, or allergy medicine. Also, women cannot use certain types of birth control pills. Herbal supplements are also off-limits. Mixing MAOIs with any of these may cause an adverse reaction.

Anti-anxiety drugs: Drugs such as benzodiazepines are very powerful. They work to fight anxiety and have very few side effects. Sleepiness is the only one that is noticeable. This medicine is only prescribed for a short period of time. Doctors are tired of giving them to former drug addicts.

Because people can easily become addicted to them, they look for additional doses to keep them going. However, if you have a panic disorder, you can use these drugs for up to a year.

In the case of social phobia, Klonpin and Ativan are used for panic disorder. One of the most common antidepressants on the market is Xanax, which is used for GAD and panic disorder.

If a person suddenly stops taking benzodiazepines, he or she may experience withdrawal; anxiety attacks may return. This is one reason why some doctors are wary of using this drug or use it sporadically.

Another anti-anxiety medicine is Busiprone, which is used for GAD. There are some side effects that include nausea, headaches, or dizziness. It is taken differently than benzodiazepines. Busiprone must be taken every day for at least 2 weeks before a person feels the effect of the anti-anxiety drug.

Beta-blockers: Beta-blockers are used to treat heart conditions. They can also be used to keep away the physical symptoms that cause anxiety disorders. Beta-blockers are used in situations such as when a person gives a speech in front of other people, a gambling blocker can be used to keep those symptoms at bay.

If you're taking medicine for an anxiety disorder, here's what you should do:

- Ask your doctor to advise you which medication would be effective for your condition.

- Ask your doctor to talk to you about how the medicine works and what the side effects of taking it are.

- Tell your doctor about other medicines you may be taking. They can interfere with the dosing of drug anxiety disorders.

Your doctor should advise you about dosage and how to take it. He or she should also advise you how to stop taking it when the time comes. With medication, some of them can trigger systems that can cause panic attacks. Doctors should always start with a lower dose and work their way up.

Chapter 8: Psychotherapy

Psychotherapy involves interacting with a mental health professional, such as a psychologist, psychiatrist, or someone who is trained to counsel about mental health problems and conditions. They can help you figure out what triggers anxiety and panic disorders. They also work to see what the best way to fight the symptoms is.

Cognitive-behavioral therapy

Cognitive-behavioral therapy, or CBT, is very effective in treating anxiety disorders. Thinking patterns are changed by the cognitive part. How people react to anxiety-related problems is the behavioral part.

People with panic disorder can use cognitive-behavioral therapy to distinguish between heart attacks and panic attacks. CBT can also be used to help them overcome social phobia. It can help them realize that not everyone is watching their every move, nor is everyone judging them.

There are techniques they can learn to use for positive exposure. These techniques will also help them to be less sensitive to anxiety triggers and symptoms.

The therapy for those who are suffering is to get them to have contact with the germs or dirt on their hands. They should wait a while before washing them. The therapist will help them deal with the anxiety that follows before they wash their hands. The more they do so, the more the anxiety fades.

If a person suffers from social phobia, their therapy would be to spend time with other people in social situations. They should resist trying to leave when they begin to feel uncomfortable. They won't feel embarrassed or feel that people are judging them.

If someone has PTSD, their therapy may be encouraging that event that caused them a lot of trauma and pain in their life. This can help lessen the fear they feel inside.

With cognitive-behavioral therapy, therapists will provide you with ways to do deep breathing and other exercises to eliminate anxiety. The exercises can help you relax in tense and stressful situations.

Phobias have been treated with behavioral therapy that forces you to expose yourself in a way that brings out your true fears and apprehensions. The face of whatever they were afraid of.

It may be looking at pictures or hearing voices on tape. It could also mean a face-to-face encounter with that person. The therapist will accompany them to support them so that they can face their fears head on.

With CBT, this therapy should connect directly with the person's anxieties and be oriented toward what they need. The only thing that will affect them is how uncomfortable they will feel due to the increased anxiety. However, that's only temporary.

This type of therapy lasts about three months to 12 weeks. It can be done individually or with a group of people who have similar conditions. For social phobia, group therapy is better because the person will have to interact with other people. For certain anxiety disorders, medication may be required for treatment to be effective.

Chapter 9: Alternative Treatments

In addition to medication and therapy, there are alternative treatments that can be used to combat these conditions in the anxiety and panic attack family.

One of the main keys to overcoming anxiety and panic attacks is to relax. That is not as easy to do as some people think. Start by concentrating and making sure you are breathing slowly and steadily.

When a person has a panic attack, one of the first things that happens is that they have trouble breathing. Sometimes they have to pant to catch their breath. The purpose here is to make your breathing even so that it slows your heart rate.

This will help the panic attack eventually go away. A person can calm down by breathing slowly. He should continue to release air from his lungs. This helps them take deep breaths and feel calmer.

Lying down with your back near a wall, bend your knees with your feet against the wall. Use one foot at a time and press against the wall. As you press down, breathe in. As you release it from the wall, exhale. Change your feet when you are doing this. Take about 15 minutes until the feeling of panic has dissipated.

Try not to think about the past. Many times, panic attacks occur because of something in the past that upset you. Look at the different shapes and colors. If you like pets, buy a small dog or cat and give it some love.

If you like fragrances, you can use aromatherapy to relieve anxiety and panic attacks. One scent that has a calming effect is lavender. There are many places where you can buy essential oils.When you feel an anxiety or panic attack coming on, smell the oil and it will work to calm you down. You can also use it as a massage oil, along with olive or grape seed oil. There are other aromatherapy oils you can use. You have to smell them to see which one you prefer.

Chapter 10: Making Your Treatment More Effective

There are independent support groups you can join. You will be able to share your knowledge and experience with those who are dealing with similar problems. There are also online chat rooms.

However, this should be done with caution. Not everything someone says about anxiety and panic attacks is the gospel. You can also seek the advice of your pastor or web minister. However, you should be sure to seek the advice of a trained mental health professional.

There are also meditation and stress management techniques. This can help those with these disorders to stay calm and focused. This can also help with your therapy. As you find ways to find peace within yourself, there are some things you should avoid using.

These include caffeinated drinks, illegal drugs, and some over-the-counter cold and sinus medications. They can actually cause the symptoms of anxiety and panic disorders.

Having your family in your life is crucial to your full recovery. They should support you and help you in any way they can. However, there may be some family members who want to tease and ridicule you.

They may tend to think it is trivial and has no merit. You may talk to them and make them understand that this is a serious illness. If they still refuse, then go ahead and find some friends who will have your back and provide the support you need.

Chapter 11: Panic Attacks Left Untreated

Panic attacks can continue for a long time, sometimes for years. This longevity can be complicated by having constant attacks.

 Symptoms include having certain phobias (fears) or leaving home, not wanting to be around other people, feeling suicidal, financial problems and substance abuse. As a result, the person may end up with heart disease.

If panic attacks are not treated, anxiety can increase and get worse. Your daily routine can be affected by attacks that don't go away. This must be addressed head-on, otherwise the person cannot be a productive citizen of society.

Chapter 12: Preventing Panic Attacks

There are ways to decrease the chance of a panic attack. You can learn to deal with them better. You must recognize the symptoms.

When the initials start, they can be others that appear. Just remember to take slow, deep breaths.

Keep lowering your anxiety level through things like exercise and meditation. Don't be in a hurry and take your time with this.

Doing it quickly can defeat the purpose. Therapy is a process that takes time and improvement will be gradual.

Don't be hard on yourself. Take it easy. Don't hit your head criticizing yourself for your condition. Be sure to avoid things like cigarettes, caffeinated teas, and carbonated drinks. That can be hard, but at least start weaning yourself slowly.

Work on not thinking about things that may have been traumatic for you in the past. These traumatic events can determine how you will react to things in the future. You can't let the past stop you from moving forward.

Make sure you maintain a loving and

supportive support system around you so you can move forward every day. Whether it's family or friends, they should be genuinely interested in helping you improve and alleviate those fears you have bottled up inside.

Chapter 13: Giving Your Support

If you're helping someone who has one of these conditions, it's very important that you're there for the long haul. It may take more than a few weeks or months for that person to get over this completely.

You should not judge or patronize the person who is suffering in any way. This is a serious matter and you should treat it as such. The worst thing you can do about anxiety and panic attacks is to be dismissive and think they can be overcome quickly. You cannot be the savior of them and solve their problem.

People who have these kinds of attacks don't think about anything except how scared they are that something bad is going to happen. The situation cannot be solved by shaking them and making them come out of it, or by waving a magic wand over them and saying "abracadabra".

Don't underestimate their actions by thinking they are pretending to act. This is serious and their actions should not be underestimated. The best thing you can do is to do everything in your power to be there as that support system.

They could feel at any moment that they are in grave danger. They feel that they cannot get out of whatever problem they perceive. That's when fast heartbeats, shortness of breath, and other symptoms come into play.

If you ignore them, you're doing more to hurt them than to help them. They depend on your support and if you decide to abandon their weakest moment, they will feel more helpless.

This can cause them to start feeling depressed and not want to do much about their situation. If they know that you are there to help them cope, then they will feel better about themselves.

You must let them go through the attack. If you try to intervene, you could make the situation worse. Let it happen and eventually they will come out of it. However, if for some reason they don't stop, call a paramedic to help you.

One thing you don't want to do is give them medication, especially if your doctor doesn't prescribe it. That will definitely cause them harm. So make sure you don't do anything to jeopardize their well-being.

There is hope for those who have been suffering for a long time with anxiety disorders and panic attacks. They need to be willing to take the step to make changes in their lives. There are other people who are suffering like you.

However, your situation doesn't have to stay that way forever. There is help out there in the form of medication and therapy. You just have to want it for yourself. The sooner you get help, the better off you'll be. Once you do, you will stop allowing these conditions to control your life.

Visit our author page on Amazon and get more **MENTES LIBRES!**

http://amazon.com/author/menteslibres

If you wish, you can leave a comment on this book by clicking on the following link so that we can continue to grow! Thank you very much for your purchase!

https://www.amazon.com/dp/B08B4BW2XL